P9-CEH-074

In the
Castle

ENGLISH HERITAGE

English Heritage is an organization that
takes care of castles all over England.
To find out more about them and about
real castles you can go and see,
visit their website at:
www.english-heritage.org.uk

Edited by Gillian Doherty
With thanks to Dr. Abigail Wheatley
for information about castles and knights

First published in 2006 by Usborne Publishing Ltd, 83-85 Saffron Hill, London EC1N 8RT, England.
www.usborne.com Copyright © 2006 Usborne Publishing Ltd. The name Usborne and the devices ♀ ⊕ are Trade Marks
of Usborne Publishing Ltd. All rights reserved. No part of this publication may be reproduced, stored in a retrieval system,
or transmitted in any form or by any means, electronic, mechanical, photocopying, recording or otherwise,
without the prior permission of the publisher. First published in America in 2006. UE. Printed in Dubai.

In the
Castle

Anna Milbourne

Illustrated by Benji Davies

Designed by Laura Parker

Have you ever visited an old, tumbledown castle...

...and wondered what it was like to live there, long, long ago?

This castle belonged to a king and a queen.
But they didn't live in it alone.

Knights lived here too,
and ladies-in-waiting...

...and horses and blacksmiths and cooks.

It was a very
busy place indeed.

The king of the castle ordered everyone about.

He sent the knights
on exciting adventures.

And when they rushed back
with tales of all they'd done...

...the king's little nephew
would long to be a knight.

But first he'd have to learn to ride...

...and fight with
a wooden sword.

He'd help a real knight get ready...

...for each
heroic quest.

Later, when he was old enough...

...and brave enough...

...the king might make him a knight too.

He'd kneel before the throne.

"Arise Sir Knight!" the king would say,
and tap his shoulders with a sword.

From then on, his job would be
to help keep the kingdom safe.

When enemies attacked,
all the knights sprang
into action.

They lifted up the drawbridge,
so no one could come in.

But the enemies swam across the moat and climbed the walls on ladders.

So the knights fought them off with swords...

...and pushed the ladders down.

Then they shot with bows and arrows...

...until the enemies
ran away.

To celebrate the victory,
the king and queen had a party.

They ate
roasted peacock
and fish with flowers...

...and honey cakes and gingerbread.

A jester clowned around and made everybody laugh.

The next day, they played jousting.

Two knights rode fast
towards each other and
tried to knock each other off.

It hurt quite a bit if you lost.

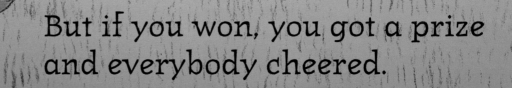

But if you won, you got a prize
and everybody cheered.

Soon, the castle went back to normal.

The king gave orders
and ruled his kingdom.

The cooks cooked and
the servants cleaned...

...and the knights did whatever they liked
until they were needed again.

That was all a long, long time ago.

But just imagine
if it weren't...